Peace Is a Pelican

poems by

Louise Moises

Finishing Line Press
Georgetown, Kentucky

Peace Is a Pelican

Copyright © 2024 by Louise Moises
ISBN 979-8-88838-659-0 First Edition
All rights reserved under International and Pan-American Copyright Conventions. No part of this book may be reproduced in any manner whatsoever without written permission from the publisher, except in the case of brief quotations embodied in critical articles and reviews.

ACKNOWLEDGMENTS

Alone; Shiny Things. *FSVAA Art Show* "Patterns" and Poetry Reading collaboration
Discovery. Sunday Morning Scrub Jays. *Soul Making Keats*
Bayside Walk in Winter. *Avocet: A Journal of Nature Poetry*
Sisyphus. *Wingless Dreamer, Sunkissed.*
A Lizard's Trek. *The Gathering 15, The Ina Coolbrith Circle*
Migrating Elk. *Tiny Seed Literary Journal*
Peace Is.. *Artists Embassy International,* Dancing Poetry, Grand Prize Winner

Publisher: Leah Huete de Maines
Editor: Christen Kincaid
Cover Art: Dennis Bayer
Author Photo: Maddie Hogan
Cover Design: Elizabeth Maines McCleavy

Order online: www.finishinglinepress.com
also available on amazon.com

Author inquiries and mail orders:
Finishing Line Press
PO Box 1626
Georgetown, Kentucky 40324
USA

Contents

Ocean Memories 1

Octopus 2

Perhaps the Dove 3

Omen 4

Message in Snow 5

Alone 6

Discovery 7

Bayside Walk in Winter 8

Winter Gardening 10

Sisyphus 11

Sunday Morning of Jays 12

Merganser Meditation 13

Fishermen 14

Contemplating Green River 15

Midwest Vision 16

The Oarsman 17

Jack Rabbit 19

A Lizard's Trek 20

Migrating Elk 21

Campsite 22

Shiny Things 23

Peace Is 24

For Scott, Wade, Maise and Vaughan Henry, whose love continues to inspire me, and for all the beautiful poets who have read and listened to my work. I am grateful for your encouragement.

Ocean Memories

You ran down the beach,
exercised muscled-legs
extending heron-like from khaki shorts,
white windbreaker flared about your arms
like the outspread wings of a gull.
Your bare feet left footprints in the sand,
slowly washed away by waves.

I played along the shore,
watched you get smaller,
chill water washed around my ankles,
splashed above my knees,
wetted rolled pant-legs, shivering,
I waited in the shallow waves.

From a half-mile off,
you turned, waved,
a blurred vision in descending fog.
You began to move towards me,
gradually your face developed
like a Polaroid photograph.

You joined me at water's edge,
took me in your arms,
heavy breath in my ear,
scent of briny air, salt-sweat of your body,
rough whiskers against my sunburnt cheeks.
        White foam lapped around our feet,
            sun sank into the sea,
                tide flowed out.

Octopus

Tiptoeing in tide-pools,
toes tickled by a tiny octopus,
      unique species, a one-of-a-kind...
                              like you, like me.
    We swim in pools of discovery,
        reach tentacles into crevices,
            risk dangerous adventures.
                In confusion, drift
                      on vast oceans of chaos,
                search the deep for meaning.

        Is it possible answers float
           just above us
           in our small rock-rimmed world?

Perhaps the Dove

Perhaps the dove meant nothing, a lone bird
lost between light reflecting windows of high rises
and sheltering green trees, her wings a flash of white
among a flock of slate-grey pigeons.

> *I stood by the window in the hospital room*
> *where he dozed, linked to life by wires and tubes.*
> *I listened for his voice.*

Perhaps the dove was just a bird passing through
morning air with no more significance than blackbirds
on the wire or the mewing, circling gulls.

> *His still face refused to awaken,*
> *oxygen hissed into nostrils, fluids*
> *steadily dripped into his failing body,*
> *vile machine blipped with false hope.*

Perhaps the dove appeared by accident,
me standing there in unexpected circumstance
looking at the sun rising over rolling hills,
exhausted after a week of sleepless nights.

> *I shook him mercilessly, laid my body beside him,*
> *pinched the loose skin on his bruised hand.*
> *Nothing except the steady hiss.*

Perhaps the dove did not flutter a message,
impossible to hear a sound of wings
through thick tempered glass.
As I stared into the empty air,
    the dove flew by the window,
        rose into the clouds
            and disappeared.

Omen

The day after I scattered your ashes
beneath our thorny rose bushes,
                an osprey circled the house,
                        your favorite bird—

                                  never before or since

      you watching over me
             as you always did
                      with your wide outspread wings.

Message in Snow

Last night snow blanketed
our old wooden deck,
an inch or more accumulated,
a fluff of white batting atop brown boards.
Silently, it fell, hushed hours lengthened by cold.
Beyond the bluff, I heard the cattle bawl
hoofing at mounds where hid last autumn's dried grass.
Grey morning dawned. Behind lace curtains,
parted for a peek, I spied a single perfect footprint
marking the mass of white, memento of early morning,
reminder of the cat that got away,
neighborhood's lonely stray,
four toes, a pad of foot
like a company logo
on a stiff white business card.

Alone

The stream floods and recedes,
leaves behind a field of clean
water-washed stones imbedded on sand:
a rubble, a multitude of rocks and pebbles
swept from eroded banks.

For miles these rocks have traveled,
washed down from mountains,
tumbled and rumbled, formed
a geological mosaic of shapes and hues:
pink feldspar, gray slate, orange calcite,
clear quartz, dark basalt, porous limestone.

Beneath the surface moisture lingers,
attracts a bright orange fritillary butterfly,
sensitive tarsus detects water.
Proboscis unfurls, tubular sucking-
organ reaches between stones
for a sustaining drink.

Two and half inches of opened wings
cast a small dark shadow on pebbles.
In a moment of sun-drenched afternoon,
a photographer captures the lone
butterfly drinking among the stones.

Discovery

My friend says, *Do you have a little extra time?*
I have something to show you. Turn left
on to the dead-end.
We sit quietly at Ookwe Park,
a small sacred space,
an ancient Ohlone shell mound
discovered during excavation of nearby underpass.

From one end of the park to the other,
a hard-packed earthen trail
curves like a river
marked with a row of etched granite boulders.

Beneath our feet, preserved in soil,
bones of ancestors, animal skeletons,
baskets, shells- many shells.
Hundreds of mounds
once ringed the San Francisco Bay,
many destroyed by development.
Today, with more awareness,
workers discover and report,
occasionally spaces preserved.

Ohlone still live in this community.
Their voices named the park: Ookwe-medicine.
Planted along the borders, native medicinal plants.
Planted too, weighty, granite boulders.
Japanese artist, Masayuki Nagase,
met with the Ohlone, studied their history,
listened to their stories, honed
their memories into solid rock.

My friend and I walk in silence,
glide hands over etched stone,
feel the shapes of waves, of fish, of shells.
Chill wind flows in from the bay,
pushes damp fog into granite crevasses,
air fills with scent of herbs.

Bayside Walk in Winter

I don my heaviest turtle-neck sweater, down jacket,
thick socks in leather hiking boots, woolly scarf...
dressed for a winter's walk along the Bay.
For fifteen minutes I briskly trot,
avoid the whoosh of speeding bicyclists,
side-step dog-walkers with extended leashes.
I watch for any form of wildlife,
nothing out and about...perhaps the cold
keeps critters in their burrows, birds hidden in shrubs.
Foghorn drones, salty scent of receding tide permeates the shore.
Mud-flat, usually teeming with wading birds,
sits silent, dark and barren.

Then four immature egrets land on a small muddy island
sticking out of sluggish green slough,
pure white feathers look like clean laundry
blown in on this chilly afternoon.
I stop running, move quietly, cautiously,
up onto the arched bridge, I lean over the railing,
stare down at four feathered friends.

Without guidance of an adult,
these small birds seem uncertain.
They stretch their necks, hunch their shoulders,
fluff their wings, shake tail feathers, strut and flaunt.
For ten minutes I delight in their curious antics,
wonder where they spent the summer.
Suddenly, three of the egrets open their wings,
take to the air, glide over the marsh,
landing one after the other in pale green reeds.
The abandoned egret walks about on stiff legs,
glances this way and that, then joins his brethren.

Wind off the Bay suddenly swirls,
bends the reeds, startles the egrets.
The birds take to the air, long legs extended.
Four immature egrets disappear around the bend.
When I arrive, there is no sign of them.
I stuff my cold hands into my pockets
and head for home, satisfied.

Winter Gardening

sun hides behind a grey shroud
aching trees bare of leaves bend
brittle twigs crack under foot
a surprise of pink roses
defies winter's dying

gloved hands dig shallow holes
prepare bare dark earth
moist from winter rain
plant bulbs in fertile ground
hopeful of spring's rebirth

trowel encounters a burial
remnants of seasons past
old bones in rich loam
digging blocked by roots
of ancient absent trees

black-backed spider scurries
hides beneath fallen leaves
green weeds defy cold
earthworms dig deeper still
avoid the scoop of a blade

cold invades painful limbs
arthritic arch of back
knees absorb moisture
air hangs in heavy chill
voice of my lover hovers

his ashes scattered here
mingled and mulched with leaves
years have not erased the vision
of his face tangled in roots
where I kneel in winter-damp soil

Sisyphus

Silvery spider, no bigger than a dime,
reaches her thread thin legs from beneath
moss matted shingles,
arches her body against the weight,
feels her way into the cold night,
she emerges to gaze skyward,
bathes in the luminosity of a full moon.

Eight knee bent legs tiptoe to the roof's edge,
she lowers herself on a fine filament,
dangles between the glowing face of the moon
and the flat, whitewashed wooden door.
Here is where she will weave.

She anchors her sticky thread to the doorframe,
clings and battles against gravity,
attaching the lines first to one side then another,
playing out strands of spider lace
into an intricate warp and woof,
her complex design shines in the moonlight
like a tapestry of rare oriental silk waiting
to collect droplets of midnight dew.

The moon sinks behind the mountain
leaving the spider to rest in darkness.
At dawn she awakens to a terrible vibration.
The whitewashed wooden door swings open
breaks the fabric of her moonlight creation,
throws her mercilessly towards the earth,
where she swings back and forth
clinging to the last remnant
of her nighttime work.

Sunday Morning Scrub Jays

A pair of blue-grey Scrub Jays
appear outside my office window,
distract me from my work.
They invade the maroon-leafed cherry tree,
hop about, lording their size over
finches, chickadees and warblers,
wee birds who flit among
moss decorated branches.

The Jays carrying in their beaks, peanuts
from some unknown source,
they pound them on the heftiest branches,
knock until the shells release
the treasure within.

On this Sunday morning,
sitting before the computer,
staring out the window,
bored by the possibility of bookkeeping,
I am gathered into the ministry
of Scrub Jays...
an invitation to devotion,
wings to the sky, a choir of soft caws,
all I can do is pray.

Merganser Meditation

Each morning around ten,
I stand on the bank of the river,
    wait for the appearance of a lone Merganser.
        She lands on the exposed boulder mid-river,
      tucks her legs beneath her rounded body,
dips her scarlet-orange bill into a fluff of breast feathers,
rusty-crest nods up and down, head swivels
to groom slate-grey feathers of her long back.
Then she stands on yellow legs,
    wiggles her pintail,
            launches into the river…
          riding low, she bobs on the surface,
          legs hidden in brown water
              drifts effortlessly on the current
                    heading down stream—
        when she reaches the bend in the river
        where rapids begin to rumble,
          she takes to the air, croaking a deep kra-kra-kra…
wings her way up stream to the rock where she began.
Standing erect, she shakes water from her wings,
        does not take time to preen,
           hurls herself back into the current
              to float once more.
Everyday for an hour or more,
        she floats and flutters
        moving with the flow.

On the edge of the river, I find a rough rock,
    sit in quiet meditation,
        marvel at her consistency,
    an avian form of yoga…
            In harmony with this floating duck,
              I find peace.

Fishermen

We meet again, my riverbank companion...
I with limber rod and pocketed-vest filled with gear,
hoping to lure a trout with a fly.
You, in feathers bluer than the sky,
balancing on a branch, bright eyes stare at the water.
A doe wanders from the willows,
steps into the shallows, bends to drink,
scaring the tiny fishes from their hiding places.
In an instant, you split the water with your beak,
rise in an arc holding a silvery fish.
I envy your grace, your precision, your fish.
You are a master of your craft, a Kingfisher!

Contemplating Green River Lands
For a painting by Wayne Thiebaud

Fabric on the land, a patchwork:
wool, muslin, corduroy, chenille
stitched together: roads, fields, a river

    harmony of tone
    softness of line
    there is no hate
    on these gentle slopes

        abundance of crops neatly furrowed
        trees without threat of falling
        river merely meanders
        sun warms each curve
        winter a figment of the imagination.

            All mankind should wish to live
            in this world of kind colors.

Midwest Visions

I stand a solitary figure
   in wondrous landscape
      watch the weather
         paint pastel horizons
            feel the weight of rocks
            that keep me from floating
            away on my reverie
In swaying grain
   insects hover and hum
      songs of a lost lover
         heat rises in waves
         wraps round my bare shoulders
         pulls me backwards

I relinquish my body to gravity
   relax onto the earth
      spread my arms in dryness
         listen to a crunch of grasses
         inhale scent of summer

Lying on my back
   sky widens
    in upper reaches of blue
      a red-tailed hawk circles
                I attach myself to his wings
                         and soar

The Oarsman

My son, in his fifty-third year,
broad of shoulder and chest,
powerful arms, tanned legs
bracing against the blue rubber raft,
gloved hands grip the long oars,
he dips their tips into the icy snow-melt
of the upper Arkansas.

My son, the oarsman,
shares the gift of the river with me,
freedom of abandoning the land,
our world is this moment,
        the *now* of the rapids

He guides us into the swirl of the river,
downstream through a surge of sounds
between tunneled rocks of Brown's Canyon
past the decaying railroad bridge,
propelled by the forces of gravity,
we descend on waves of clarity,
red rocks pinned against the sky,
water-washed boulders create rushing rapids.
We spin, dip and dive,
behind us snowcapped Rockies,
        before us a whirl of water.

My son reads the river,
pulls on the oars, thrusts us into the raging staircase,
through flumes, past rocky lions
and profiles of sandstone figures,
expertly into holes and around bends we plunge.

In the bow, I sit white-knuckled, screaming..
I peer down into a hole in the river, face my fear.
We fall, water washes over the raft and over me.
My son's wide-mouthed laughter
    booms in harmony with the roar of the river.
At the end of the run, near the take-out where the water rests,
    I'm proud of you Mom..
his voice floats above this quiet place.

Jack Rabbit

In heated afternoon
      Jack Rabbit and I
      the only ones on the trail.
His majestic ears spoil
an effort at camouflage
      he senses my presence
      stands perfectly still
unblinking in harmony with brambles
a totem of the high desert

Around us, scent of dry
      summer grasses, pungent aroma
      of sunbaked sage, an incense
benediction in this tabernacle
of southwestern landscape
      unseen song sparrow trills
      clear, pleasing notes, light and slightly husky
soloist at the altar
no need of a choir
      A lizard, so thin, I almost miss him,
rests in the shadow of a boulder

I lean on my walking stick
wipe the sweat from my forehead
sip from my water bottle
linger,
unwilling to break the spell.
I take a few cautious steps
      keep my eye on the rabbit

            I could stand here for hours
                maybe even days
              yet I know
                    in this life
                          there is only moving forward.

A Lizard's Trek

A lizard, the color of Kaibab sandstone,
skips and scampers
across an array of Navajo blankets
displaying a rainbow of native crafts
meant to tempt the browsing tourists.

The lone lizard roams over tightly woven baskets,
mounting and descending a row of silver necklaces,
burning his feet on the sun warmed amulets of hematite,
splayed toes race across a tangle of turquoise bracelets,
around the curvature of a hand coiled pot etched
with images of corn maidens.

He mounts a soapstone sculpture of an iguana,
matching reptile for reptile.
From his perch, he stares down at his prey:
a singular, leggy, lean, red ant, who stops and waits,
just out of reach, knowing somehow,
the length of the lizard's sticky tongue.

Then like a stage magician, the ant vanishes down a hole
too small for the lizard's girth.
The lizard performs a disappointment dance
swaying from side to side, executing four fine pushups,
then scurrying for safety in camouflage.

From beneath an overhanging rock,
the lizard watches as the bronze-skinned Navajo
offers a bracelet to a pale woman
with soft round arms.
Money and smiles are exchanged,
Neither Navajo nor woman
are aware that a lizard
stepped upon the bracelet
leaving sacred hidden messages
with his toes.

Migrating Elk

Elk
Last night
crossed the road
as they have done
each year since I moved
to this mountain retreat

Elk
Left hoof prints
on the muddy trail
last night
cows called to their calves
in high pitched squeals

Elk
Crossed the road
last night, a portent
of an early winter
left hoof prints
on the muddy trail

Elk
Have returned
each year since I moved
to this mountain retreat
crossed the road
left hoof prints

Elk
Crossed the road
last night
migrating up the mountain
cows called to their calves
in high pitched squeals

Now I know the herd is safe.

Campsite

At dusk
I yield to the peaceful landscape,
contemplate the setting sun,
how she paints the horizon
with a watercolor wash of pink and lavender.
Cooling night softens heated day.
Crescent Moon and Venus meet like elicit lovers,
linger above the mesa, unable to embrace.
As darkness descends,
distant coyotes howl for their mates.
Beside the campfire,
I fall asleep,
dream of a harmonious world.

Shiny Things

Scrub Jay balances on the banister,
flash of some shiny thing in her beak,
a babble to decorate her nest. Oval glass
casts moving prisms on the wall:
crimson, orange, yellow, pale green.

Squirrel with a banner of red tail
sits upright on the fence. Two agile
paws hold a treasure, a glass stone
pulled from my planter, inedible. He drops
the shiny thing into dew-damp grass.

Clear glass vase, vessel for violets,
ovals of reflecting stones sink to the bottom,
a weight beneath slender green stems.
Shiny things sparkle in the water
like bulging eyes of goldfish.

Four-year-old grandson sits at the table,
holds a handful of colorful glass beads.
Together we count the shiny things...
one to twelve, more precious than gems,
they clatter into grandma's
blue glass bowl.

Peace is...

Peace is a sunset seen through a veil of fog,
lacy waves lapping sandy shore, alone with the tide,
salty fragrance of the sea, listening to the mantra
of crash and recede, crash and recede on into infinity—

Peace is a pelican framed against an aqua sky,
soaring along the shore, unaware of wars,
winging above waves, a prehistoric vision—
would that I could fly on wings of a pelican.

Peace is the discovery of an ancient oak,
gnarled, bent, enduring, an elder with stories to tell.
Listen: snap of twigs, crack of branches, rustle of grasses,
around depths of roots—a history.

Peace is a small girl on a big horse
rounding a barrel in a dusty rodeo arena—
a crowd of friends, family, perfect strangers, all cheering,
unity of the moment, the many as one.

Peace is being alone with a waterfall:
chill splash of rushing, roaring water,
fragrance of pine, swoop of swallows singing—
standing beneath a cascading curtain of water.

Peace is witnessing a birth of monarchs—
from cracked chrysalises, wet stain-glass wings
struggling to open and close, thin black legs
clinging to feathery fronds of milkweed.

Peace is a prayer whispered in shadows,
a large clanging bell, angle of ceiling,
scent of incense, flicker of candles—
Peace is finding a church within your heart.

Peace is a solitary figure in a high desert landscape,
scent of heated sage, sky as large as it can ever be,
a rocky line where earth meets clouds,
then a simple gesture—a wave of love.

LOUISE MOISES, a graduate of San Jose State, was born and raised in the San Francisco Bay Area, where she still resides. She has been a teacher, storyteller, puppeteer, retail clerk, and the owner of an antiquarian bookstore, along with being a wife, mother and grandmother. Now widowed, she enjoys traveling with her cat in her 23-foot RV, exploring out–of-the-way places that inspire her writing.

Her poems been recognized with awards from the literary divisions of the San Mateo, Marin and Alameda County Fairs, the Ina Coolbrith Circle, Artists Embassy International, and Soul Making-Keats, and have been published in a number of online venues and printed anthologies, including *High Shelf Press, A Gathering, Sunkissed, California Quarterly, the Write Launch, Ariel, Pinole Writers Group, Wingless Dreamer,* and *The Avocet*.

Louise has been a featured reader at various venues. Some of her performances can be viewed on YouTube. Along with writing, she enjoys reading, dancing, singing and gardening. According to Louise, every day is a new poetic adventure.

www.ingramcontent.com/pod-product-compliance
Lightning Source LLC
Chambersburg PA
CBHW022059080426
42734CB00009B/1422